Surviving

MOUNT EVEREST

AN INTERACTIVE EXTREME SPORTS ADVENTURE

by Blake Hoena

CAPSTONE PRESS
a capstone imprint

You Choose Books are published by Capstone Press,
1710 Roe Crest Drive, North Mankato, Minnesota 56003
www.mycapstone.com

Library of Congress Cataloging-in-Publication Data is available on the Library of
Congress website.

ISBN: 978-1-5157-7169-2 (library binding)
ISBN: 978-1-5157-7173-9 (eBook PDF)

Editorial Credits
Nate LeBoutillier, editor; Bobbie Nuytten, designer; Eric Gohl, media researcher;
Katy LaVigne, production specialist

Photo Credits
Alamy: Christian Kober, 49, LatitudeStock, 12; Getty Images: Adventure Nomad/
Kenneth Koh, 36, 72, Andrew Bardon, 61, Jason Maehl, 22; iStockphoto: Daniel
Prudek, 91, 102, fotoVoyager, 4, 42; Newscom: imageBROKER/Peter Giovannini,
27, 33, 96, Mountain Light/Galen Rowell, 1, Reuters/Navesh Chitrakar, 101, www.
billstevensonphotography/Bill Stevenson, 10, 52, ZUMA Press/Bogati/Nawang
Sherpa, 77, 81; Shutterstock: Anton Rogozin, 6, 108, Daniel Prudek, 16, 107, Galyna
Andrushko, cover, Kondoruk, 56, PlusONE, 64, Vector1st, back cover, Vixit, 87

Printed and bound in Canada.
010382F17

TABLE OF CONTENTS

ABOUT YOUR ADVENTURE

YOU are about to take part in one of the most difficult adventures. Mount Everest is a very challenging climb. Most people who attempt to reach its summit fail. Oftentimes it is because of the weather or a random accident or an illness caused by the altitude. Other times it is because of poor decision-making. Each year, a number of climbers even lose their lives.

Your choices will guide the story and determine whether you make it to the summit. How will you proceed? Will you ascend with caution or charge forward for glory?

Turn the page to begin your adventure.

CHAPTER 1

GEARING UP!

The plane's overhead speakers crackle, and you hear the pilot announce, "We are nearing our destination of Kathmandu, Nepal's capital city."

You peek out your window. The towering peaks of the Himalayan Mountain Range fill the horizon.

Kathmandu will not be your final stop. You and your climbing partner, Charlie, have decided to test yourselves on the world's highest peak. Mount Everest rises just over 29,000 feet above sea level.

While climbing Everest is an exciting challenge, your adventure comes with its dangers.

Turn the page.

The weather can be brutally cold. Avalanches have sent tons of icy snow crashing down on climbers. There is also little oxygen to breathe high up on the mountain. Reaching Everest's summit is a feat that only the hardiest and luckiest climbers can achieve.

You and Charlie had made arrangements through a Nepali trekking agency. Upon your arrival, you are to meet your lead guide at your hotel.

He introduces himself by saying, "My name is Manish, but call me Mani."

Mani is short and lean. He speaks with confidence and is always smiling.

"During parts of the climb, we will have other Sherpas join us," he says. He adds, chuckling, "They will help you, but they won't carry you."

Six months earlier, you and Charlie filed for the permits needed to climb Mount Everest. Mani's trekking agency will supply camping gear, special climbing equipment, and food. But Mani sent a list of things, from insulated boots to goggles, for you and Charlie to bring. He inspects everything. Gear must be in prime condition to lower the risk of anything breaking or wearing out. Before your adventure truly begins, you need to pick a climbing route. Mount Everest is a huge mountain with more than a dozen possible paths to its summit. Many are too difficult to consider. The majority of climbers take one of three routes.

South Col is the most popular, but it starts off with the dangerous Khumbu Icefall. It is the route taken by New Zealander Edmund Hillary and Sherpa Tenzing Norgay back in 1953. They were the first to summit Everest.

Turn the page.

It is often necessary to use ladders to cross crevasses on Everest.

For the Northeast Ridge route, you will have an easy drive to Base Camp. Back in 1922, George Mallory made the first-ever attempt to climb Mount Everest from the north. He failed, partially because this route is exposed to the mountain's harsh temperatures and winds.

Then there is the West Ridge route, which is the most difficult of the three. A U.S. team consisting of Willi Unsoeld and Tom Hornbein first conquered this route back in 1963. Since then, only a handful of climbers have been able to match their feat.

Which route will you attempt to climb?

South Col route, turn to page 13.

Northeast Ridge route, turn to page 43.

West Ridge route, turn to page 65.

Lukla airfield is the point of arrival for many Everest adventurers.

CHAPTER 2

SOUTH COL ROUTE

The next day, you leave Kathmandu on a twin-engine prop plane. It takes you to Lukla, a small village near the base of Mount Everest. You spend the night there.

When you arise the next morning, you join Mani for breakfast.

"How'd you sleep?" he asks.

"Didn't," Charlie replies. "Too nervous."

"I'm nervous too," you say.

"A little hike will settle your nerves," Mani says. "We have nearly 40 miles to Base Camp."

Soon, you are on your way.

Turn the page.

The trail is well traveled but not easy. Your backpack is heavy with gear, and the winding path has many ups and downs.

About mid-morning you cross the Dhudh Kosi River on a rope suspension bridge. It bounces and sways with every step you take. Just after noon, you reach the village of Monjo.

"Should we spend the night here?" Mani asks. "Or can you make it to Namche Bazaar, the next village?"

You have the beginnings of a slight headache, and it might not be a bad idea to rest. But you have only hiked a few miles. At this pace it will take you a week to reach Base Camp.

To stay in Monjo, go on to page 15.
To continue on to Namche Bazaar, turn to page 17.

You tell Mani that you are not feeling well and would rather rest up.

"The altitude is weakening you," he says. "Kathmandu is about 4,600 feet above sea level. Monjo is twice that, and Base Camp is more than 17,000 feet. Your body needs to adjust. Best to take things slow."

And the going is very slow. The next day, you hike to Namche Bazaar and rest there. Each day you trek only a few miles before spending the night in one of the villages along the way.

After more than a week, you reach Base Camp. Colorful tents are spread out on a large, rocky plateau. It is the first of several camps that you will stay in during your climb up Everest.

Mani leads you to your tent.

Turn the page.

Base Camp at Mount Everest features tents and prayer flags.

"Rest up," he says. "Tomorrow, we climb the Khumbu Icefall."

Both you and Charlie are exhausted after the long hike to Base Camp, and the difficult part of the climb has not yet begun. Do you get up early the next morning to tackle the Icefall or do you sleep in to get some extra rest?

To get some extra rest, turn to page 19.

To get started early, turn to page 21.

"I think I could do a few more miles," you tell Mani confidently.

Charlie nods in agreement.

"Okay," Mani says. "Let's go."

You head out, but it isn't long before your head starts throbbing. You feel a knot of queasiness in your stomach. As you are about to step onto a rickety suspension bridge, your feet come to a halt. The thought of it swaying under your feet makes you want to vomit.

"You okay?" Charlie asks.

You shake your head.

"What's wrong?" Mani asks.

"I've got a headache," you say. "I feel like I'm going to throw up."

Turn the page.

"Could be altitude sickness," Mani says. "Your body is not used to the thin mountain air. We should have spent the night in Monjo."

Luckily, you are not far from the village. You make it back leaning on Mani most of the way.

In a couple of days, you feel better. A week later, you reach Base Camp. It is a village of colorful tents spread out on a rocky plateau, and the first of several camps that you will stay at during your climb.

During the long hike to Base Camp, you learned that mornings start off cold. But once the sun rises, the weather warms. The next morning, do you sleep in to take advantage of the warmer temperatures, or do you get an early start?

To get some extra rest, go on to page 19.
To get started early the next morning, turn to page 21.

You had a long hike to reach Base Camp, and you struggled to adjust to the altitude. You feel like you deserve some extra rest.

When you crawl out of your tent, the sun is shining. It is surprisingly warm.

Mani waits for you with two Sherpas, Daya and Pasang.

First, you hike to the Khumbu Icefall, a glacier of slowly shifting ice and snow. Its constant movement has created a landscape crisscrossed with deep crevasses.

The going is difficult, but at least the weather is nice. By noon, you reach an area of the Icefall nicknamed Popcorn. It is a maze of towering ice pinnacles called seracs. As you hike, you hear a loud crack.

"What was that?" Charlie asks.

"Must be one of the seracs," Mani says. "If it gets too warm, they can collapse."

"We should have started earlier," Daya says.

Suddenly, there is another booming crack, only this one is much closer.

"Look out!" Pasang warns.

Everyone turns to see one of the seracs teetering as its base cracks and pops.

"Run!" Mani shouts.

The serac topples in your direction. But in this icy landscape, you can't run fast enough. The giant column crashes down on you and Daya, crushing you both under tons of ice and snow.

THE END

To follow another path, turn to page 11.
To learn more about Mount Everest, turn to page 103.

The next morning, you wake before the sun rises. You and Charlie are excited to begin, so you want to get an early start. When you find Mani, there are two Sherpas with him.

"This is Daya and Pasang," Mani says. "They will climb with us today."

It's a short hike to the Icefall. This slow-moving glacier looks more like a raging river that was frozen in place. Its constant shifting has created a treacherous landscape crisscrossed with deep chasms. Towering pinnacles of ice called seracs form where the crevasses meet.

As you strap crampons to the bottoms of your boots, Mani pats you on the back.

"Good thing we got an early start," he says. "The sun and melting ice can make the Icefall a dangerous place."

Turn the page.

During this climb, and most other climbs, you are hooked by a safety rope to one of the Sherpas. You go with Daya, while Charlie pairs up with Pasang.

The going is tough. You follow a zigzagging trail that skirts around chasms and weaves through seracs. All the while, you climb slowly upward. Camp 1 is just over a mile and a half away, but it takes you all morning to get there.

The Khumbu Icefall can be a treacherous obstacle for climbers.

At Camp 1, you are in for a big shock.

Mani asks, "How do you feel?"

"Exhausted," you say.

"I'm beat," Charlie gasps.

"Tomorrow we go back down," says Mani

"What?" you ask, shocked. "We're not giving up yet."

"No, no, no," Mani says. "We will make this climb several times. Your body needs a chance to adjust to the altitude."

The next morning, you head back to Base Camp. Then the following day, you hike up the Icefall again. Mani has you do this several times.

Then one day, Mani announces, "Tomorrow we cross the Western Cwm."

Turn the page.

The Cwm is a large, U-shaped valley. At one end sits Camp 1. Toward the other is Camp 2. Just beyond that lies the Lhotse Face.

The next morning, when you step out of your tent, you are greeted by three smiling Sherpas. They wear ball caps and heavy sweatshirts, and they have sunscreen smeared across their faces. You are bundled up tightly in your parkas and balaclavas.

"It'll be a bright, sunny day on the Cwm," Mani says. "You don't need to bundle up like penguins."

Then your group heads out.

Once the sun pokes above the surrounding peaks, sunlight reflects off the snowy walls of the valley. The light is blinding and heats up the Cwm.

As you hike, you come to a deep chasm that is more than 20 feet wide.

"Look, a bridge," Charlie says with a snort. He points at several aluminum ladders that have been strapped together and laid across the chasm.

"That's scarier than those suspension bridges we crossed on our hike to Base Camp," you add.

You could try crossing the precarious ladder-bridge, hoping it holds you and your heavy backpack. Or, you could head toward the middle of the valley and walk around the chasm.

To cross the ladder bridge, turn the page.
To walk around the chasm, turn to page 29.

You stand at the edge of the chasm. In either direction, it stretches as far as the eye can see.

"Finding a way around this could take all day," Mani says.

"Then let's cross this bridge," you say boldly.

You go first. The ladder is anchored in place with ropes. There are also guide ropes stretching across. You clip a carabiner to one of them.

As you take your first step, the ladder shifts. Then you take a second step. Through the ladder's rungs, you see the bottom of the chasm hundreds of feet below.

You take a third step and a fourth. The bridge sags in the middle where the ladders are attached.

Charlie urges you on, saying, "You can do it!"

Step after cautious step, you make it across.

Crossing a crevasse by ladder on the Western Cwm can be an adventuresome experience.

Mani walks across as if he were on a morning stroll. You continue on and cross more chasms on the way. You reach Camp 2 in time for lunch.

Mani has you cover the Western Cwm several times over the next few days. While it helps your altitude adjustment, it also builds your confidence.

Finally, Mani says you are ready to climb the Lhotse Face. This steep slope is covered in packed ice and snow. You need to reach Camp 3, high up near the top of the slope. From there, the South Col ridge leads to Everest.

Turn the page.

Two ropes hang down the Lhotse Face. A line of climbers has gathered to climb up one. Climbers above head down the other.

"Where are Daya and Pasang?" Charlie asks.

"They have gone ahead of us with supplies," Mani says.

When it is your turn, you clip a carabiner to the guide rope. You kick, and your crampons bite into the icy slope. You push yourself up with one foot and then kick the wall with your other foot.

After 200 feet, you reach the end of the guide rope, and a new one begins. You need to connect a carabiner to the new rope before continuing your climb. How do you do it?

To unclip the carabiner you've been using and hook it to the new rope, turn to page 31.

To grab a new carabiner to hook it to the new rope, turn to page 33.

You step to the edge of the chasm and glance at what's far, far below.

"That's a long ways down," Charlie says.

"And I don't trust that bridge," you say. "Let's go around."

You follow the chasm toward the middle of the valley. It slowly narrows, and eventually ends.

"Look!" you say. "We can get around it."

As you hike around the end of the chasm, the ground suddenly drops away. You stepped onto a snow bridge, which hid the crevasse. The Cwm's intense heat had weakened the bridge.

Your fall is stopped by the sudden jerk of your safety rope. Dawa stopped your fall. You bang into the side of the chasm and feel a sharp pain in your shoulder.

Turn the page.

"You okay?" Mani shouts down to you.

"I'm not sure," you reply.

Once you are pulled to safety, your shoulder begins to throb with pain.

"Let's get you back to Base Camp," Mani says.

There, you learn that you have fractured your collarbone. You will be unable to continue. So the next day, you begin the slow and painful trek back to Lukla.

Maybe next time.

THE END

To follow another path, turn to page 11.
To learn more about Mount Everest, turn to page 103.

You kick your feet into the slope. The crampons bite and grab. With one hand, you unclip your carabiner. With the other hand, you hold onto the guide rope.

You struggle to clip the carabiner to the new rope. So you let go of the rope to use both hands. As you reach up, the ice shifts under your feet. You are thrown off balance and begin to slide down the steep slope.

You crash into Charlie and don't stop until you reach Mani.

"You okay?" Mani asks.

You feel battered and bruised but nod.

After clipping you to the guide rope, Mani goes to check on Charlie.

"My leg," Charlie cries out.

Mani lowers Charlie to the base of the slope. A doctor at Camp 2 says that Charlie appears to have a fracture. With Charlie unable to continue on, your adventure is over.

"I'm sorry," you say to Charlie.

"You can make it up to me," Charlie says.

"How?" you say.

"By carrying me down the mountain."

Despite your disappointment, you laugh.

THE END

To follow another path, turn to page 11.
To learn more about Mount Everest, turn to page 103.

You know that you always want to be connected to a guide rope. So you have a second carabiner on your climbing harness. You clip that one to the new rope. Then, and only then, do you unhook from the other rope.

Soon, you are back to climbing. It is slow and exhausting work. By time you near the top, your legs shake from the effort.

Turn the page.

Reliable ropes can be climbers' best friends.

When you near the top, you see Daya and Pasang. They help you to your tent at Camp 3.

The next day, Mani's plan comes as no surprise. You climb down the face, only to climb back up the following day. A couple of days later, Mani meets you outside your tent.

"Are we climbing back down again?" you ask.

Mani shakes his head. "Time to push for the summit," he says. "You will need these."

He holds out two oxygen masks. You spent weeks adjusting to the altitude, but you can still feel the lack of oxygen in the air. Your breath is labored, and you feel tired. The lack of oxygen will only increase farther up the mountain. If a person's body does not get enough oxygen, the muscles and organs can stop working.

Mani helps you put the masks on. He connects them to a bulky oxygen tank that will be strapped to your back. As you begin climbing, you feel a little more energized despite the added weight.

You start out with a steep ascent. After a while, the trail flattens as you walk over windblown rock. You have reached the South Col, the ridge that stretches from Lhotse to Everest. By time you reach Camp 4, you and Charlie practically crawl to your tent.

"Sleep with your masks on," Mani tells you. "That will help you rest. We have another long climb tomorrow."

Timing is crucial. Mani says it will probably take you 12 hours to reach the summit from here. When do you begin tomorrow's climb?

To leave at midnight, turn to page 39.
To leave at sunrise, turn to page 36.

On most days, Mani has you get up just before sunrise. So you stick to that plan. That way, daylight is not far behind. And once the sun pokes over the surrounding mountains, the weather gets milder.

"We're now up in the Death Zone," Mani says as you are getting ready. "We don't want to spend much time up this high."

Mani sets a steady pace. After a couple of hours, you take a break at a flat spot called the Balcony. Mani checks your oxygen tanks.

You start up the Southeast Ridge, a steep slope that leads to the South Summit, a small peak. On this climb, you use a jumar, a device that clamps onto the guide rope so you can pull yourself up. The going is slow. Exhaustion creeps in.

When you near the top of the ridge, you notice people climbing down. Mani stops to talk with their lead guide. Then he looks at his watch and shakes his head.

"It's past noon," he says. "The weather is turning. We must head back."

"How far away are we?" you ask. You can see the main peak just up ahead.

"At least two hours," Mani says. "We won't have time to get back to camp, and it's deadly up here after dark."

Turn the page.

If you had left at midnight, maybe you would have reached the summit. But now it is too late. You have to turn back or put your life at risk.

"Let's play it safe," Charlie says. "We can always try one of the other routes."

You nod and admit defeat.

The climb down turns out to be more difficult than the climb up. The temperature drops as the wind picks up. If not for the Sherpas, you and Charlie could not have made it back to camp.

While you failed to reach Everest's peak, you still had a great adventure. You made it farther up the mountain than most climbers. Best of all, you lived to tell about it.

THE END

To follow another path, turn to page 11.
To learn more about Mount Everest, turn to page 103.

Mani wakes you about midnight. Winds are gusting, and the frigid air stings. You begin to second-guess your decision. But Mani urges you onward.

"We don't want to stay up this high too long," he says.

The area above 26,000 feet is called the Death Zone. At this altitude, both the cold and lack of oxygen are deadly.

Mani sets a fast pace. You struggle to keep up. But Daya helps you with difficult parts of the climb. You peek back to see Pasang helping Charlie. Without the Sherpas, neither of you could navigate parts of the icy trail.

At just over 27,000 feet, you reach a flat area called the Balcony. Here, Mani swaps out your oxygen tanks for new ones.

Turn the page.

You look up at the triangle peak of Everest. It looms large, a couple of thousand feet above.

"I think we can make it," Charlie says, giving you a nudge.

"Yeah," you say. "I think we can, Charlie."

From the balcony, you head up a steep ridge. It is some of the steepest climbing yet, and you rely heavily on a jumar. This device clamps onto the guide rope so you can pull yourself up.

After a couple of hours, you reach the South Summit. From this small peak, you have a clear view of the path leading to the summit.

Next, you reach the Hillary Step, named after Edmund Hillary. It is a 40-foot rock jutting out of the mountainside.

"Follow me," Daya says.

He climbs the crack between the rock and the mountain, and it is precarious. To one side is a thousand foot drop off. To the other, a wall of rock.

Every time you or Charlie falter, the Sherpas urge you on. You focus on planting one foot in front of the other until you hear prayer flags flapping in the wind.

Daya guides you over to the rock the prayer flags are tied to. You walk up and touch it. Charlie does the same.

Mani pats you both on the backs. "You have made it!" he shouts.

You straighten your back, standing at the top of the world.

THE END

To follow another path, turn to page 11.
To learn more about Mount Everest, turn to page 103.

Base Camp high in the Khumbu Valley

CHAPTER 3

NORTHEAST RIDGE ROUTE

The next step in your journey starts with a flight to Lhasa, China. Two days later, you hop on a bus to Shigatse. You spend a night there before continuing on to another small village.

On the following day, the road ends at the Rongbuk Monastery. This temple sits near Base Camp, which is the first of many camps you will stay in during your adventure.

"We're at 17,000 feet," Mani says. "More than halfway up."

"Yeah, the easy half," Charlie says.

You smile.

Turn the page.

At Base Camp, tents spread out on a rocky landscape and streamers of prayer flags flap in the wind. They provide the only color in the bleak landscape.

When you head out from Base Camp, you hike along a valley carved by the Rongbuk Glacier. Just after noon, you turn into a side valley formed by the East Rongbuk Glacier. You stop at a small camp to eat lunch.

"We could spend the night here," Mani says. "Or, we could continue to Advanced Base Camp."

To stay, go on to the next page.
To keep going, turn to page 48.

"Perhaps we should stay and rest up," you say.

"Good choice," Mani says. "We've climbed about 3,000 feet today. We don't want to rush up the mountain. You could get sick."

Charlie looks down at his untouched meal. "Yeah," he says, "I haven't been able to eat much."

"Lack of appetite is a sure sign that you are being adversely affected by altitude," Mani says.

While at the small camp, you see Sherpas continuing up the mountain. They lead yaks carrying heavy packs.

"They have lived here all their lives," Mani explains, looking on with pride. "They are used to the thin mountain air, unlike you."

The next morning, Mani leads you toward a moraine nicknamed the Magic Highway.

Turn the page.

As you reach the tail end of the East Rongbuk Glacier, ridges of ice rise up around you. The Magic Highway creates a path through them.

About midday, you reach Advanced Base Camp. Mani leads you to your tent.

"You must rest up," Mani says. "There will be a difficult hike tomorrow."

The next morning, your tent shudders from the wind. You step outside and are blasted by frigid air. You and Charlie walk over to the mess tent to join Mani. He sits with two Sherpas.

"Meet Yash and Nabin," Mani says. "They will climb with us to Camp 1."

You continue to hike alongside the glacier. The trail is rocky with a slight incline.

What makes things difficult is the wind. It cuts through your outer layer of clothing. You wear goggles to protect your eyes from the swirling snow.

Eventually, you need to cross the glacier.

"This weather is getting bad," Mani says. "It might be best to head back."

On the other side of the glacier, you face a steep climb up to 23,000 feet. You do not want to admit defeat this early in your adventure, but you wonder about Mani's suggestion.

To keep climbing, turn to page 51.
To turn back, turn to page 54.

"Let's keep going," you tell Mani.

The hike from the small camp starts off easy. But as you continue, a knot of queasiness forms in your stomach. Your head begins to throb. At one point, you double over, feeling sick.

"You okay?" Charlie asks.

You shake your head no.

Mani walks over. "Are you okay?" he asks.

"No," you admit.

"It's the altitude," he says. "Lhasa is around 12,000 feet, and we're now above 20,000."

"It's like we've climbed a small mountain since leaving Lhasa," Charlie adds.

Mani nods, and then says, "Best to take things slow to adjust. We'll head back to camp and rest."

Taking an occasional rest is an important part of any serious climb.

It takes a couple of days for you to fully recover and make it to Advanced Base Camp. From there, you will head to Camp 1. On the morning you are to leave, Mani introduces you to two other Sherpas.

"Meet Yash and Nabin," Mani says. "They will climb with us today."

You exchange pleasantries.

Turn the page.

With Mani, Yash, and Nabin, you and Charlie hike alongside the East Rongbuk Glacier. Hours later, you prepare to cross the glacier. On the other side is a steep slope that leads up to Camp 1.

Before you start up, you notice that the weather is worsening. The clouds darken, and the wind whips up. Swirling snow forces you to put on your goggles.

"We will have a storm," Mani says.

"Should we turn back?" Charlie asks.

You only have a few hundred feet to climb, but you worry about the weather. It is not good to get caught in a storm while on Everest's slopes. But you do not like the idea of giving up, either, when your adventure is just beginning.

To keep climbing, go on to the next page.
To turn back, turn to page 54.

"I don't want to give up yet," you tell Mani.

"Yeah, we've barely begun," Charlie adds.

Mani nods. "Then let's keep going."

Each of you strap crampons onto your boots. Then you set out across the glacier. You trek through a maze of jutting snow and ice.

On the other side of the glacier, the mountain rises steeply. Guide ropes lead up. You clip a carabiner to one of the ropes.

After a couple hundred feet, you stop at the edge of a deep chasm. An aluminum ladder stretches across the crevasse. It is anchored down by ropes. A number of safety ropes have also been strung across.

"That's a bridge?" Charlie asks.

Mani smiles and nods.

Turn the page.

You clip a carabiner to a safety rope. Then you take a step onto one of the ladder's rungs. A hundred feet below, you see the very bottom of the chasm.

You take another step, then another. The ladder starts to shake.

"Steady," Mani says.

But you cannot stop shaking, whether it is from being cold, your exhaustion, or the weather. When a gust of wind slams into you, you lose your balance. You tip over the side of the ladder. As you fall, stars light up your vision.

You are jerked to a stop. The safety rope has stopped your fall.

You feel woozy and don't remember exactly what happens next. You're dimly aware of Mani crawling out onto the ladder to pull you to safety. Your mind drifts in and out of the moment as Mani hauls you back to Advanced Base Camp.

At camp, a doctor examines you. She finally determines that you received a concussion from your fall. You pushed yourself despite the horrible weather, and as a result you have been injured.

You cannot risk further damage to your health. All too soon, your Everest Adventure has come to an end.

THE END

To follow another path, turn to page 11.
To learn more about Mount Everest, turn to page 103.

"I'm not sure," you say.

"Let's not give up now," Charlie adds.

"We aren't," Mani says. "We will climb up and down this part of the mountain several times. If we don't make Camp 1 today, we will try again tomorrow."

True to his word, Mani has you make another attempt the following day. The weather is not as harsh, and you make it to Camp 1. Then the very next day, you head back down to Advanced Base Camp. Each time you make the round trip, you feel a little less winded.

Then one morning, gusts of wind send snow and ice flying off rocks. You bundle up before heading over to the mess tent. Mani is waiting for you.

"Ready to head up to Camp 2?" Mani asks.

"Yeah, sure," you reply.

"It's time for some new scenery," Charlie adds.

Yash and Nabin soon join you.

Camp 1 is at the base of a ridge called North Col. It leads up to Everest's Northeast Ridge, which then leads up to the summit. About a third of the way up North Col, at just under 25,000 feet, is Camp 2.

Guide ropes are anchored along the ridge. But before clipping onto one, you must decide whether to strap crampons onto your boots. These metal teeth will give you extra traction if the trail is icy.

To put on the crampons, turn the page.
To climb without your crampons, turn to page 58.

For the climb up to Camp 1, you needed crampons to cross the Rongbuk Glacier. So you assume you will need them today.

But the wind races over the ridge, carving away the snow and ice. Much of the rock is now bare, making the metal teeth of the crampons feel clumsy. You slip and stumble as you climb.

Crampons help climbers ascend ice-covered rock faces.

At one point, the rock you step on shifts. You trip. Reaching out to break your fall, you feel a sharp pain in your wrist.

"Ow!" you cry out.

Nabin rushes over. "You okay?" he asks.

You clutch at your wrist, which has exploded with pain.

Mani and Charlie join you.

"Let's climb down to Advanced Base Camp," he says. "A doctor can check your arm."

At Advanced Base Camp, the doctor informs you that you have suffered a fracture. Everest is an incredibly difficult climb. With a broken arm, you will not be able to continue on.

THE END

To follow another path, turn to page 11.
To learn more about Mount Everest, turn to page 103.

You decide you do not need the crampons. The wind is whipping up and scraping the rocks bare of ice and snow. Crampons would be pointless and even dangerous on bare rock.

During the climb, you use a jumar. You reach forward with this device, and it tightens on the rope. Then you pull yourself up. It is slow, exhausting work, and you don't reach Camp 2 until after noon.

When you crawl into your tent, Charlie plops down on the ground.

"Wow, that was rough," he gasps.

Over the next week, you climb the slope between Camp 1 and Camp 2 several times. Once, you even head all the way back to Advanced Base Camp. But with each trip, the climb becomes easier and you gain confidence.

One day while at Camp 1, Mani holds a sheet of paper with the current weather reports.

"Looks like we have good weather for the next few days," Mani states. "Let's try for the summit."

Mani explains that tomorrow you will climb up to Camp 2. The next day, you will head to Camp 3. From there, you will push ahead for the summit.

When you head out, you realize that "good" weather is still frigid. But at least you make it to Camp 2 with no problems.

The next morning, Mani hands you and Charlie oxygen masks.

"You will need these," he says. "Camp 3 is almost 26,000 feet. It is near the Death Zone. There is little oxygen there."

Turn the page.

The mask hooks to an oxygen tank, which you carry strapped to your back.

Today, you only need to climb about 1,000 feet, but it feels like you are running a marathon. Your arms shake from the effort of pulling yourself up by a jumar.

The winds constantly buffet you, causing you to stumble and nearly fall. Your toes and fingers feel numb from the cold. You doubt you could have made the climb without the extra oxygen energizing you.

After about six hours, you see a handful of tents on a narrow ledge. The Sherpas help you and Charlie to yours. You collapse inside. That night, Mani tells you to sleep with your oxygen masks on so that you do not get sick from the low air pressure at this altitude.

Oxygen masks are a necessity for climbers high up in the mountains.

The next morning, you head up the remaining part of the North Col ridge. As before, you use a jumar to pull yourself up. After a few hours, you reach Camp 4, where a few tents sit on a small ledge.

Turn the page.

At more than 27,000 feet, few climbers stay up this high for long. This camp is mostly a rest stop. You eat a snack, drink some water, and Mani checks your oxygen. He has a stash of full tanks at Camp 4.

"Okay," Mani says. "Are you ready? Next, we will climb the Three Steps."

You look at Charlie. Charlie nods. It seems you're both feeling a shared determination.

The first step is at around 28,000 feet. It is made of several large boulders. You hook a carabiner to a guide rope and slowly pull yourself up.

The second step is nearly vertical. Ladders have been rigged up to help with the climb. Only, the ladders are on the side of the step. That means you are exposed to the winds, and have a drop of thousands of feet should you fall.

The third step is the easiest. From there, you hike up the steep slope toward the summit. After about an hour, you see prayer flags flapping in the breeze. They have been tied to a large rock straight ahead of you. Nabin guides you over to it. Then Charlie joins you.

You grab your friend's hand and raise it high up into the air.

"We made it!" you shout.

You have done what few others have even attempted. You have summited the top of the world's tallest mountain!

THE END

To follow another path, turn to page 11.
To learn more about Mount Everest, turn to page 103.

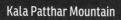

Kala Patthar Mountain

CHAPTER 4

WEST RIDGE ROUTE

Most climbers attempt to reach Everest's peak using the South Col route or the Northeast Ridge route. But you want more of a challenge, and the West Ridge will provide that. There are not any established camps up on the West Ridge, and therefore you will spend more time at high elevations in the thin air.

Before heading to Base Camp, you need to decide how to get up to the West Ridge. You could start on the Nepali side of the mountain. This is the route Willi Unsoeld and Tom Hornbein of the United States took back in 1963. Or you could start on the Chinese side of

Turn the page.

the mountain. Back in 1986, a Canadian team established this route. Sharon Wood was among the team members, and she became the first North American woman to reach the summit.

It's an exciting decision for the most challenging of routes. In which country will you start your climb?

To start in Nepal, go on to the next page.
To start in China, turn to page 71.

Nepal it is. The next day, you hop on a twin-engine prop plane. It will take you to Lukla, a small village near the base of Mount Everest.

You get an incredible view of the Himalayas, flying above some of the world's tallest peaks. You also get a bit of a scare during the landing. Just before the runway there is a thousand-foot drop. Turbulence causes the plane to jump up and down. But it makes a safe landing.

Charlie leans over and says, "Mani says this is the most dangerous airport in the world."

"Yeah, I can see why," you reply.

That night, Mani tells you what to expect next. "It's nearly 40 miles to Base Camp," he explains. "It will take a week to hike there."

"Bet I could do it in two days," Charlie brags.

Turn the page.

"Sure," says Mani. "But then I would be carrying you back down." He's not smiling.

"What do you mean?" you ask.

"It's the altitude," says Mani. "Kathmandu is about 4,500 feet above sea level. Lukla is nearly twice that, and Base Camp is more than 17,000 feet. We take things slow so your body can adjust to the thinning air, or you could become ill."

You have read about altitude sickness. Mild cases cause a loss of appetite, restless sleep, and headaches. Bad cases can cause difficulty in breathing and confusion—not good when trying to climb up a dangerous mountain.

The next day, you hike a few miles to the village of Monjo. The following day, you hike a few more miles to Namche Bazaar. It is there that you get your first view of Everest.

From the ground, Everest's pyramid-shaped peak dominates the horizon like an arrow pointing toward the heavens.

In a few more days, you reach Base Camp, the first of several camps you will use on your climb.

"Rest up," Mani says. "Tomorrow, we climb the Khumbu Icefall."

Early the next morning, Mani greets you with two Sherpas by his side. "This is Tenzin and Sanjiya," Mani says, gesturing. "They will climb with us today."

The Icefall is a slow-moving glacier. Its constant shifting has created a landscape of deep chasms and towering pillars of ice called seracs.

"It's a mile and a half to Camp 1, where we will spend the night," Mani says.

Turn the page.

You attach crampons to your boots. The metal spikes provide extra traction on the ice and snow.

You feel like an ant in a world made for giants. You skirt around deep chasms and weave your way around seracs.

Then you reach a section of the Icefall known as the Popcorn. It is a maze of seracs. Mani leads, followed by Charlie and Sanjiya, and then you and Tenzin. At one point, you take a step and hear a booming crack. You sense the danger, but where is it coming from? Is something crashing behind you or is the ground giving way in front of you?

To run forward, turn to page 74.
To back up, turn to page 82.

The next step in your adventure begins with a flight to Lhasa, China. From there, you have a three-day bus ride to Base Camp.

Mani shows you to your tent, where you drop off your gear. You spend the next two days hiking around camp, but there is not much to see in the bleak, rocky landscape.

When you leave Base Camp, you hike up a valley carved out by the Rongbuk Glacier. About noon, you stop at a small camp.

"We will spend the night here," Mani says.

As you and Charlie eat lunch, you see Sherpas leading yaks up the valley. Mani goes to chat with them. Then he lets you know that they are carrying supplies to your next camp farther up the valley.

Turn the page.

The following day, the going gets more difficult as you reach the tail end of the Rongbuk Glacier. You strap crampons to the bottom of your boots. These metal teeth provide extra traction on the icy terrain.

East Rombuk Glacier

About midday, you reach a small camp near the base of Everest's west shoulder. Several Sherpas come out to greet Mani. He brings two of them over to you.

"Meet Tenzin and Sanjiya," Mani says. "They will climb with us." Gesturing at the half dozen other Sherpas and then the slope nearby, he says, "The others will help carry gear up the mountain. We could not carry all of it ourselves."

The next morning, you hike over to the slope with Mani, Charlie, Tenzin, and Sanjiya.

Mani points out two possible routes up to the ridge. One is windblown with a mix of ice and rock along the trail. The other looks just as difficult, only it is out of the wind, somewhat, and covered in snow.

To take the ice and rock path, turn to page 77.
To take the snowy path, turn to page 80.

The rest of your group is safe up ahead. So the danger must be behind you. You lunge forward. You only glance back when you hear a second, louder crack.

Tenzin races toward you. "Run!" he shouts. "Run fast!"

Behind him, one of the seracs teeters. You need to get out of its path.

You move as fast as you can manage over the icy terrain.

Bam!

The earth shakes. An explosion of ice and snow throws you to the ground.

Tenzin rushes over to you.

"You okay?" he asks.

You lift your head and nod.

"Whoa!" you hear Charlie shout. "That was really scary."

"Yeah," you say. You're thankful all is okay.

Despite the close call, you continue.

Icy cliffs block your way. Sometimes a trail of ladders forms a path up them. Other times, you use an ice axe to pull yourself up.

Hours later, the terrain levels out. You see Camp 1 up ahead. Mani leads you to your tent, and you take a needed rest.

You are surprised the next day when Mani says you are climbing back down the Icefall.

"Why?" Charlie groans.

"The altitude," Mani explains. "We'll hike between camps until you are acclimated to the thin air."

Turn the page.

That's exactly what you do the next couple of days. You hike back and forth between Camp 1 and Base Camp. Then Mani has you hike through the Western Cwm to Camp 2. This U-shaped valley is protected from high winds, so on clear, sunny days, it can get incredibly warm.

You spend the next couple of days hiking back and forth across the Cwm. It is difficult work but helps you understand the terrain of the huge mountain.

Then one day, you wake to snow. Big flakes swirl about in the wind. You and Charlie join Mani in the mess tent.

"What do you think of the weather?" he asks. "Should we climb up to the West Ridge or head back to Camp 1?"

To climb to the West Ridge, turn to page 83.
To return to Camp 1, turn to page 85.

Loose, slippery snow worries you, so you choose the path with exposed rock.

Mani leads the way. Since this is not a well-used route, he has a difficult job. He anchors guide ropes as he climbs. Once a section of rope is secured, the rest of the group follows.

You clip a carabiner to the rope and then start to climb.

Turn the page.

You kick at the icy slope. Your crampons bite into the ice, giving you a foothold. Before pushing up, you swing your ice axe overhead, embedding it into the mountain. You use it to steady yourself.

As you climb, you notice that the ice is brittle. This is often true of old, exposed ice. At one point, you swing your ice axe. When it hits, the ice shatters. Some rocks come loose. You move out of their way. But as they roll past you, Charlie is not quick enough. One slams into his shoulder. He slips down the slope before being jerked to a stop by the guide rope. Sanjiya quickly climbs over to help him.

"He needs to go down," Sanjiya yells.

Mani and Sanjiya help Charlie down the mountain. You can tell something is wrong. Charlie's arm hangs loosely at his side.

"We have to go to Base Camp," Mani says. "There's a doctor there."

You eventually learn that Charlie's shoulder got dislocated. His arm is now in a cast. With your friend unable to continue, your attempt to climb Mount Everest ends.

THE END

To follow another path, turn to page 11.
To learn more about Mount Everest, turn to page 103.

"Let's go that way," you tell Mani, pointing to the snowy path.

"That's a good route," he says. "The snow acts like glue, holding rocks in place. Some might come loose if we climbed the other route."

Mani takes the lead. His job is difficult because he has to set the guide ropes. He anchors them in place with ice screws. Once a section of rope is set, the rest of the group heads up.

There are few footholds or handholds. You rely on your crampons for footing and use an ice axe to steady yourself.

The climb takes most of the morning. Mani pulls you up when you reach the top. You have an incredible view. In one direction, the world drops away into a wide mountain valley. In the other, a jagged ridge leads up to the pyramid-shaped summit of Mount Everest.

"We are above 23,000 feet," Mani says. "Only 6,000 more to go."

"The fun is just beginning," Charlie says.

You hike a little farther along the ridge. Mani finds a flat ledge where you set up Camp 3.

The following day, you climb back down the West Shoulder. More gear needs to be carried up before you can continue on.

Turn to page 87.

You stop, thinking the ground is about
to crumble under your feet. You slowly inch
backward.

There is another booming crack behind you.

You turn to look. Tenzin rushes toward you.

"Come on!" he shouts.

Behind him, one of the seracs teeters as its
base splinters and cracks apart.

Tenzin tugs at your arm, trying to get you
moving. But you are too slow. The serac crashes
down on you and the Sherpa with a thunderous,
deathly boom.

THE END

To follow another path, turn to page 11.
To learn more about Mount Everest, turn to page 103.

Other than the snow, the weather seems fine, and you are getting tired of hiking up and down the mountain.

"Let's climb!" you say.

"Yeah!" Charlie adds.

"Okay," says Mani.

Mani leads the way. You and Tenzin follow him, and Charlie and Sanjiya climb last.

You kick one foot into the side of the icy slope. The metal crampons bite into the ice, giving you a solid foothold. Between the ice and snow, it is difficult to find any handholds, so you use an ice axe. You reach up and bury its point into the side of the slope. Holding onto the axe steadies you as you use your leg to push yourself up. You repeat this process over and over again.

Turn the page.

As you climb, the snow keeps falling. It makes it difficult to see Mani above you.

Oddly, you hear a rumble.

Then you hear Mani shout. He scrambles down the mountain.

"Avalanche!" he screams.

On your precarious perch, there is nowhere for you to go.

You look up as a wall of snow and ice and rock barrels into you. You are ripped from the side of the mountain. While the fall does not kill you, you are buried alive and pinned under packed snow. Your breaths grow ever shorter. There's just no air for you to breathe. The world turns dark.

THE END

To follow another path, turn to page 11.
To learn more about Mount Everest, turn to page 103.

"With all this snow, I think we should climb back down to Camp 1," you say.

"Seriously?" Charlie says. "Again?"

"Heavy snows can cause avalanches," Mani says.

"Then Camp 1 it is," Charlie says with a sigh.

Despite the snow, you have an easy climb down to Camp 1.

The next day, when you return to Camp 2, you hear that there was an avalanche. No one was hurt. But if you had been climbing up to the West Ridge, who knows what would have happened.

When you finally head up to the West Ridge it is a difficult path. You climb a steep, icy slope. Luckily, this route has been used in the past.

Turn the page.

Some guide ropes are already anchored to the slope. Others need to be replaced because of the avalanche.

The pyramid-shaped summit of Everest lies along a jagged ridge from where you stand. It does not seem that far away, less than three miles. But that distance can fool you.

You still have nearly 6,000 feet to climb to reach the summit.

You set up Camp 3.

The following day, Mani has you climb back down to Camp 2. He does not want you spending too much time up on the West Ridge, not until you are more acclimated to the altitude. Also, more supplies need to be brought up before you continue up the mountain. You agree, though it gets tiresome making the same climbs and descents.

One day, while at Camp 2, you see Mani talking to a couple of Sherpas. He turns to you and Charlie and smiles.

"Camp 4 is ready," he says. "And we should have good weather for a few days. Want to try for the summit?"

"Yeah!" you say, and Charlie nods excitedly.

The next morning, you set out before the sun rises. You have climbed up to the West Ridge a couple of times and guide ropes are in place. You make it to Camp 3 easily.

Turn the page.

The next day, Mani gives you and Charlie oxygen masks.

"You will need these," he says.

"But I thought we were acclimated to the altitude," Charlie says.

"No one gets used to being up this high," Mani says.

He helps you and Charlie with your oxygen masks. The masks connect to a tank that you strap onto your back. It is heavy and cumbersome, but you are surprised at how much easier it is to breathe with the mask.

That day you hike to Camp 4. Along with setting up the camp, the Sherpas anchored guide ropes along the way. They make the going easier. You climb to about 25,000 feet. Then you find a small ledge with two tents.

As you hunker down in your tent, Mani tells you to keep the oxygen masks on.

"Even when we sleep?" Charlie asks, and Mani nods.

The next morning, there's a decision to make.

"There are two routes from here," Mani says. "We can keep following the ridge or climb the Hornbein Couloir."

Following the West Ridge is the most direct route, but it is more exposed to the elements. Where you stand now, winds whip about, and the swirling snow is nearly blinding. You also feel the tingle of cold in your toes, fingers, and the tip of your nose. The couloir is a gully along the north side of the mountain. Following it means a much steeper climb, but less exposure to the elements.

To follow the West Ridge, turn the page.
To follow the Hornbein Couloir, turn to page 94.

Mani takes the lead. He blazes the trail, and the rest of the group waits for him to anchor a guide rope.

As you wait, you hop up and down to try and stay as warm as possible. You wear heavy wool socks and insulated boots. You also have thick mittens and a glove liner under them. But the wind races over the ridge, and the cold cuts through your clothing.

When the guide rope is set, you are thankful to get moving. The movement helps warm you up. But the joints in your fingers ache as you grab onto the guide rope.

During a break, you say to Mani, "I thought we were going to have nice weather."

He laughs and says, "For Everest, no storms is nice weather."

Charlie seems to be doing no better. You see him clapping his hands together to warm them.

Sometime in the afternoon, you reach a flat spot at about 27,500 feet. There, the Sherpas set up tents.

Turn the page.

"We will rest here," Mani says, "before pushing to the summit."

You and Charlie duck into one of the tents. You shiver from the cold, and your fingers ache. Even lighting a fire to heat up water for tea is a struggle.

"What's wrong?" Charlie asks.

"I can't get my fingers to work," you say.

"Let me see them," Charlie says, reaching for your hands. "The tips are grayish."

Just then, Mani peeks inside your tent. "Are you ready—?" he starts but turns to you and says, "Let me see your feet."

"I can't really feel them," you say.

"They are warm to the touch," Mani says. "Not good. Frostbite is setting in."

"Is that bad?" you ask.

"Depends," says Mani. "Would you prefer to keep your fingers and toes?"

"Can't play guitar in our band without fingers," Charlie says, trying to get you to smile.

While you might be able to reach the summit, the risk of frostbite is too great. You decide to head back down the mountain before your fingers and toes get any worse. Otherwise, you might not be able to climb down.

THE END

To follow another path, turn to page 11.
To learn more about Mount Everest, turn to page 103.

You duck over onto the north side of the mountain. You follow a rocky ledge to the base of the Hornbein Couloir. There, you set up a couple of tents.

"Let's take our rest here," Mani says. "We will leave at midnight to try and reach the summit by noon tomorrow."

Despite the bitter cold, you manage to get a few hours of sleep. It is dark out when you set off again.

The Hornbein Couloir offers some protection from the elements, but it starts off as a steep, 45-degree angle. The higher you climb, the steeper it gets.

Mani takes the lead. He anchors guide ropes as he goes. The rest of your group follows when the ropes are set.

The going is slow and tiring. You have to use a jumar to pull yourself up the guide rope.

At one point, the couloir closes in around you. It narrows to about shoulder width. You continue in these cramped quarters. Finally, about 1,000 feet from the summit, the couloir ends. You stand on a flat, snow-covered ledge.

"Just a little farther," Mani urges.

You look up to see the summit, still looking far away.

"We can do it!" Charlie says, and you nod.

You are cold and exhausted, and you are not sure how much more of this you can take. But you are so close.

Mani blazes a zigzag trail up the last section of mountain. Step by step, you force your way up.

At this point, you focus on the excitement of reaching the summit. Without that goal driving you, you would collapse.

Summit ridge of Mount Everest

You reach the summit at midday. The view from the top of the world is stunning. Even white-capped mountains, which loomed over you down at Base Camp, seem small from so high up.

You high-five Charlie and shout, "We did it!"

After taking some photos, Mani says it is time to head back down.

"The weather will get worse as the day wears on," he says.

You had a difficult climb up. Now it is time to head back down. You can take the way you came, which is the route you know. Or you could follow the unfamiliar South Col route down. This is the route that the majority of climbers use when summiting Everest.

To follow the West Ridge back down, turn the page.
To follow the unknown trail down, turn to page 100.

Since you already know the West Ridge route, you decide it is safer.

You easily reach the snowy ledge above the Hornbein Couloir. There, you understand what Mani meant when he said the weather can turn as the day wears on. The wind whips up, and your toes and fingers tingle from the cold.

The climb down the couloir is more demanding than the climb up. When the gully narrows, you can't see where you are placing your feet. You stumble and slip, banging your knees against the rock. It is nearly dark by time you reach the bottom of the couloir.

"This is taking too long," Mani says. Then he checks everyone's oxygen. "We will run out of oxygen before reaching Camp 4."

When that happens, your difficult climb down becomes impossible. You cannot breathe in enough oxygen to keep your muscles moving.

At one point, Mani sends Tenzin and Sanjiya ahead. He hopes they can reach Camp 4 and return with full tanks.

The three of you hunker into the side of the mountain. But this is your second night in what is called the Death Zone. Above 26,000 feet, with the cold and lack of oxygen, the human body starts to shut down.

Huddled together with your friend and Mani, you fall asleep shivering. You suffer a peaceful death as you never wake.

THE END

To follow another path, turn to page 11.
To learn more about Mount Everest, turn to page 103.

From the direction of the South Col Route, you see other climbers. They high-five you as they walk to Everest's summit. They head back down, as you are about to do too.

"Let's follow them," you say.

You faced a very challenging climb, with little support. You are cold and exhausted, so the more well-traveled route seems the better option.

After a few hours, you reach a small camp on the South Col. This is Camp 4 for those taking this route.

A Sherpa walks up as you enter the camp. "You make it?" he asks.

Both you and Charlie nod vigorously.

"Good, good!" he shouts. "I have a tent set up, and food and hot tea for you."

The interior of a tent is a welcome setting on Everest.

While it took you nearly a month to reach the summit, you are back at Base Camp in a couple of days. There, you are treated like a hero. The West Ridge is a route few others have conquered. Other climbers gather around to listen to your story.

THE END

To follow another path, turn to page 11.
To learn more about Mount Everest, turn to page 103.

CHAPTER 5

MOUNT EVEREST

The tallest peak in the world was not always called "Everest." In Nepal, people referred to it as Sagarmāthā, a name that can be translated to mean "goddess of the sky." The Chinese know it as Zhumulangma Feng, among other names.

In the mid-1800s, the British government sent George Everest to survey the land from southern India to northern Nepal. This task included mapping the Himalayan Mountain Range. Everest estimated that the range's tallest peak was 29,002 feet above sea level. That is not far off from the mountain's currently accepted height of 29,035 feet. Originally it was called Peak XV, but in 1865, the mountain was renamed after Everest.

The first attempt to climb Mount Everest occurred in 1922. British mountaineer George Mallory took part in this expedition. When asked, "Why climb Everest?" he famously replied, "Because it's there." The expedition failed, mostly due to poor weather conditions. But Mallory's party did reach a record height of 26,980 feet. That was higher than anyone had ever climbed on any mountain in the world.

In 1924 Mallory and partner Andrew Irvine made another attempt to climb Everest. This expedition ended in tragedy when both Mallory and Irvine disappeared high up on the mountain. No one knew exactly what happened to them or if they had reached the summit, as their bodies could not be found. Not until 1999, that is, when Mallory's body was found, frozen solid, at 27,760 feet. Irvine's still has not been recovered.

The first confirmed summit of Everest occurred in 1953. New Zealander Edmund Hillary and Sherpa Tenzing Norgay reached its peak from the Nepal side of the mountain. No one reached the summit from the Tibetan side until 1960. A Chinese team consisting of climbers Nawang Gombu, Yin-Hau, and Wang Fu-zhou claimed to have achieved that goal.

Since these historic summits, thousands of people have tried to climb Mount Everest. Hundreds succeed every year, and a handful perish. Those who die near the top of the mountain, in the Death Zone, are left to serve as landmarks for future climbers. It is too dangerous and too difficult to retrieve their bodies from such altitudes.

From the first successful attempts until today, most climbers use the aid of Sherpas.

The term "Sherpa" refers to an ethnic group of people who lived on the Tibetan side of the Himalayas. But political turmoil and warfare forced most of them to migrate to Nepal.

Living in the Himalayas has acclimated Sherpas to high altitudes. This made them invaluable porters and guides to early expeditions. They were seen as strong and hard-working, and also good-natured and kind people. Once the Mount Everest fad began, Sherpas earned a worldwide reputation for their mountaineering skills. Few climbers are able to summit Everest without their aid.

While tourism has helped Sherpas financially, those in mountaineering have dangerous jobs. Nearly a third of those who die on Mount Everest are Sherpas.

Despite the dangers and hardships it presents, attempting to summit Everest is viewed by many as one of the most exciting and challenging adventures a person can undertake. It tests climbers' physical and mental limits. Reaching Everest's peak at the top of the world is an accomplishment that needs more that just skill and toughness, but also determination mixed in with some luck. Standing at the top of the world and seeing the incredible view is its own, rare reward.

DANGERS of EVEREST

Avalanche

When a sudden, enormous flow of snow slides down a mountainside, an avalanche is underway. Avalanches are very unpredictable and provide little or no time for avoidance. As recently as 2015 a massive earthquake and avalanche caused 15 deaths at Base Camp and the cancellation of the climbing season.

Weather

The weather is famously unpredictable on Everest. Winds that blow up to 100 miles (160 kilometers) per hour and temperatures that can drop to minus 75 Fahrenheit (minus 25 Celsius) can kill.

Falling

At such extreme heights, objects falling means trouble. Falling rock, ice, snow, and — yes — even climbers can lead to injuries and even death.

Other Climbers

The sheer number of mountaineers on Everest during climbing season can be a hazard, especially when climbers are inexperienced and get in each other's way.

GLOSSARY

altitude sickness (AL-tih-tood SIK-ness)—an illness caused by lack of oxygen at high altitude; symptoms include loss of appetite, restlessness, headaches, difficulty in breathing, and confusion

acclimate (AK-lih-mayt)—to adjust

carabiner (ka-ra-BEEN-uhr)—a metal ring with a spring; used to connect and hold ropes

col (KOL)—the lowest part of a ridge that connects two mountain peaks

couloir (kool-WAHR)—a steep mountain gorge

crampon—(KRAM-pahn)—metal spikes which attach to boot bottoms

cwm (cwm)—a bowl-shaped basin carved by glaciers

jumar (JOO-mahr)—a tool attached to a rope that aids in climbing; also called an ascender

moraine (mohr-AYNE)—streaked ridges of dirt and rock formed by glaciers

serac (suh-RAK)—a towering pinnacle of ice

Sherpa (SHUHR-pah)—a member of a people living in the Himalayas well-known for expert mountaineering skills

OTHER PATHS TO EXPLORE

◈ Sherpas are key members of almost every successful team that climbs up Everest. But for them, it is a job, rather than a goal, to help other climbers get to the top. How would the task of reaching Everest's summit be different if you were supporting other climbers?

◈ Sherpas help climbers in many ways. They guide climbers, carry supplies up the mountain, and assist with climbing. But some hardcore climbers attempt to summit Everest without the help of Sherpas. What would it be like to climb up one of the routes covered in this book without the supports of Sherpas or guides?

◈ Currently, there are about 20 routes up Mount Everest, with the South Col and Northeast Ridge routes being the most popular. Every few years, a team of climbers tries to establish a new route up the mountain. What would this be like?

READ MORE

Athans, Sandra.K. *Tales from the Top of the World: Climbing Mount Everest with Pete Athans.* Minneapolis: Milbrook Press, 2013.

Medina, Nico. *Where is Mount Everest?* New York: Grosset & Dunlap, 2015.

Rajczak, Kristen. *Climbing Mount Everest.* New York: Gareth Stevens Publishing, 2014.

Herman, Gail. *Climbing Everest: How Heroes Reached Earth's Highest Peak.* New York: Random House Children's Books, 2015.

INTERNET SITES

Use FactHound to find Internet sites related to this book.

Visit *www.facthound.com*
Just type in 9781515771692 and go.

INDEX